9/18

Biotech
Careers

Tom Streissguth

ReferencePoint Press®

San Diego, CA

About the Author

Tom Streissguth has authored more than one hundred books in many different subjects, including geography, history, biography, sports, and current events. He attended Yale University, where he majored in music, and has worked as a teacher, editor, and journalist. In 2015 he founded the Archive, an online collection of historic journalism, as a resource for students, educators, and researchers.

For more information, contact:
ReferencePoint Press, Inc.
PO Box 27779
San Diego, CA 92198
www.ReferencePointPress.com

Picture Credits:

Cover: Billion Photos/Shutterstock.com
  6: Maury Aaseng
12: Steven Debenport/iStockphoto.com
37: mediaphotos/iStockphoto.com
47: alvarez/iStockphoto.com
70: Reptile8488/iStockphoto.com

LIBRARY OF CONGRESS CATALOGING-IN-PUBLICATION DATA

Name: Streissguth, Thomas, 1958– author.
Title: Biotech Careers/by Tom Streissguth.
Description: San Diego, CA: ReferencePoint Press, Inc., [2019] | Series:
  STEM Careers | Audience: Grades 9 to 12. | Includes bibliographical
  references and index.
Identifiers: LCCN 2018013486 (print) | LCCN 2018014406 (ebook) | ISBN
  9781682824283 (eBook) | ISBN 9781682824276 (hardback)
Subjects: LCSH: Biotechnology—Vocational guidance—Juvenile literature. |
  Biotechnology industries—Vocational guidance—Juvenile literature. |
  Biotechnologists—Juvenile literature.
Classification: LCC TP248.218 (ebook) | LCC TP248.218 .S77 2019 (print) | DDC
  660.6023—dc23
LC record available at https://lccn.loc.gov/2018013486

Contents

Biotechnology: Combining Science and Medicine

Although Red Mountain High in Mesa, Arizona, is an ordinary school in most ways, its science students have something to brag about: they can work and play in a full-scale biotechnology laboratory.

The lab has prep rooms similar to those used by professional researchers. It also has a clean room, with filtration equipment donated by a pharmaceutical company. Students can design their own research using their knowledge of chemistry, physics, math, and biology. Red Mountain students have published scientific papers, spoken at conferences, and presented their work to executives at biotech companies.

"Students work with different enzymes, artificial DNA replication, DNA analysis and culturing plants or bacteria," explains student Abigail Mann in an interview for an article on MyNews Mesa.com. One project took Mann north to Oak Creek Canyon and the town of Sedona, where she worked with the Oak Creek Watershed Council on a disease-causing strain of *E. coli* bacteria, present in the creek's waters. Mann's research got noticed by Arizona State University, which extended a grant of $1,000 to fund her work.

Improving Human Lives

Biotechnology is the marriage of technology with biology, with useful applications in medicine, agriculture, genetics, and zoology. Biotech companies have created thousands of new products that improve and extend human lives, ensure the safety of the food supply, and provide breakthroughs in genetic research. In this sector, the United States is a global leader, with the largest and most successful companies concentrated on the East Coast and in California.

Not many years ago, today's biotech products would have made great subjects for a science-fiction movie. Biomedical engineers are creating fully functional artificial organs that replace damaged or diseased organs inside the body. They are developing drug-release mechanisms in the form of a skin patch—no injection necessary. Drug companies are producing medications that work at the level of DNA, the strand of proteins within each cell that controls the body's form and function.

In these ways and so many more, the biotechnology industry is improving lives. Many biotech workers are researching new drugs or therapies. Others are designing equipment such as artificial limbs or digitized voices to be used by patients. A major part of the biotechnology workforce is engaged in scientific research, product testing, or clinical trials of new drugs and therapies. Those interested in what is considered pure science often work with advanced computer software that analyzes chemical compounds and molecules. And some in the biotech world spend time with patients in hospitals or medical clinics introducing new therapies to heart patients or those battling cancer.

A Variety of Requirements

With the various jobs in biotech, there are a variety of requirements. Some positions require only a certificate course at a vocational or technical college. Some employers require a bachelor's degree with a science major, and others demand a master's degree. A background in biology, chemistry, health sciences, or physics is helpful. Many students following a premedical course decide to pursue a career in biotechnology rather than take the long, expensive road through medical school. Some positions require certification or licensing. Others are so new that state and local governments have not yet created licensing requirements for them.

Biotech Careers

Occupation	Minimum Educational Requirements	2016 Median Pay
Biochemist and biophysicist	Doctoral or professional degree	$82,180
Biological technician	Bachelor's degree	$42,520
Biomedical engineer	Bachelor's degree	$85,620
Epidemiologist	Master's degree	$70,820
Genetic counselor	Master's degree	$74,120
Health and safety engineer	Bachelor's degree	$86,720
Medical scientist	Doctoral or professional degree	$80,530
Microbiologist	Bachelor's degree	$66,850
Veterinary technologist and technician	Associate's degree	$32,490
Zoologist and wildlife biologist	Bachelor's degree	$60,520

Source: Bureau of Labor Statistics, *Occupational Outlook Handbook*, 2018. www.bls.gov.

There is another very important, common requirement for most biotech jobs: a sense of scientific curiosity. Biotech workers are interested in the functions of the body, and most have a strong desire to heal disease and improve lives.

Many Avenues to Employment

There are many avenues for those starting out in biotechnology to find employment. As in many other fields, networking is important. Professional associations offer job boards, counseling, and contacts. Many companies use professional recruiters for top executive positions or internships to scout for entry-level technicians and engineers. College professors mentor promising students, guiding them in a career path suited to the student's own abilities and interests. Volunteer opportunities offer experience in working directly with the public.

One of the most popular job search methods is the science job fair. It is a favorite way for biotech companies and jobseekers to find each other. At a job fair, company representatives take résumés and interview candidates. They answer questions about their company's history, and they may have material available on its latest products and research. Major biotech companies, including Amgen, Genentech, XOMA, and Bristol-Meyers Squibb, set up their booths and complete, on average, two to five new hires at every job fair.

In an online article published by the *Scientist*, Christos Richards comments on the many opportunities in the field: "Right now, the marketplace is becoming glutted with offerings of biotech and pharmaceutical job fairs." Richards is the founder of Career Connections, which stages fairs in many different employment sectors. Steve Campbell, president of another job fair company that specializes in biotech, reports in the same article that "the beauty of a job fair for the job candidate . . . is he or she can come and conduct a pretty sizable job search under one roof in a few hours and really know where they stand. That might take several weeks to do via the post office."

Job fairs are not the only way to find employment in the biotechnology industry, of course. Candidates can apply directly to companies, respond to website ads, work through scientific associations, meet employers who recruit on their school campus, or request information and direction from career advisers.

Healthy Prospects

The range of career interests among biotechnology employees is also very wide. Among big biotech companies, there are thousands of well-paid jobs in the nuts and bolts of any business: finance, marketing, and sales. Many of these positions offer independence, good pay, and an opportunity to climb the ladder to an executive position. And interest in biotechnology among venture capital firms and other investors is extremely high. This means that the most creative engineers and researchers in the field have an opportunity to fund start-ups and develop a thriving business of their own.

Along with the abundance of jobs—and the promising futures they hold—the most exciting aspect of this sector is the sense of constant discovery. Biotechnology is a field of breakthroughs and new developments. Workers in the field share a sense of wonder at the giant steps their fellow researchers and technicians are taking toward longer life and better health.

Genetic Counselor

Genetic Counselor

Minimum Educational Requirements
Master's degree in genetics, biology, or related scientific field

Personal Qualities
Ability to understand medical and genetic research; strong interest in hereditary disease; talent for explaining complex medical concepts to clients; empathetic understanding of client concerns

Certification and Licensing
Required in some states, with new licensing rules under consideration in others

Working Conditions
Indoors in hospitals, clinics, physician's offices, medical laboratories, outpatient care centers, and university research centers

Salary Range
From $45,540 to $104,370, with a median annual salary of $74,120 as of 2016

Number of Jobs
Approximately 3,100 as of 2016

Future Job Outlook
Faster-than-average growth rate of 29 percent through 2024

What Does a Genetic Counselor Do?

Genetic counselors work in the health care industry advising patients on their risk for genetic diseases. To do this, genetic counselors study the medical histories of the patient and the patient's family. They use family trees and pedigree drawings, which trace the occurrence of a specific illness through a family. Genetic counselors also rely on tests that reveal the structure of the patient's DNA. This substance is present in the cells of the body and is passed on from parents to offspring. Mutations (changes) in DNA, or damage to the chromosomes that contain the body's DNA code, may cause diseases such as cystic fibrosis, hemophilia, and epilepsy.

Using test results, genetic counselors can identify the risk of specific illnesses such as cancer. In the last few decades, researchers have identified genes associated with certain diseases. Mutations in the genes *BRCA1* and *BRCA2*, for example, are associated with breast and ovarian cancers. A worried patient who has these cancers in her family can take a test that analyzes these genes and predicts the patient's chances of contracting the same illness.

Some genetic counselors specialize in prenatal conditions. Using DNA analysis, they can advise expectant mothers on the risk of birth defects in an unborn child. Genetic counseling can also be useful for parents of young children. An underlying genetic condition may be responsible for slow development, autism, seizures, and even obesity. Helping parents and children through the psychological demands of testing—even helping them decide whether they want to test in the first place—is a key part of the job.

In an interview on the National Society of Genetic Counselors website, Brenda Finucane remarks on her experience as a genetic counselor: "I feel like a bridge as a genetic counselor between the science that is advancing very rapidly, and the people and the families on the front lines of these diseases." Much of the fascination of the job lies in the fact that each patient is unique, with individual circumstances that demand a different approach in every case.

A genetic counselor spends much of the day talking with clients and patients, going over test results, and discussing the best way to prevent or treat illness. In an online *U.S. News & World Report* article, Joy Larsen Haidle, a genetic counselor with the Humphrey Cancer Center in Robbinsdale, Minnesota, describes the impact the job can have on patients: "This conversation helps a patient feel more empowered with the information, rather than a gene or the cancer being in control."

Some people who come to genetic counselors may simply be curious about their family's health history. DNA test kits can reveal the inherited risk of specific conditions such as baldness, hypertension (high blood pressure), diabetes, or lactose intolerance. If the test results worry the patient, the counselor can refer him or her to a medical doctor for further tests and treatment.

How Do You Become a Genetic Counselor?

Education

To prepare for a genetic counseling career, high school students study biology and genetics. A course in psychology and any experience in a counseling role or as a health-related volunteer also helps students gain an understanding of the field. As college students, future genetic counselors usually major in biology, physics, general or organic chemistry, or genetics.

The first master's degrees in the field of genetic counseling were awarded by Sarah Lawrence College in New York in 1971. At the end of 2017, there were twenty-nine universities in the United States (and three in Canada) with accredited programs in genetic counseling.

R. Lynn Holt, a genetic counselor with the biotech research firm Hudson Alpha, holds a bachelor's degree in microbiology with a minor in genetics and a master's degree in genetic counseling. On Hudson Alpha's website, Holt explains how students can get exposure to the career during college: "It is important that you gain experiences during undergraduate school that will prepare you. . . . People will often shadow a genetic counselor, volunteer for a crisis hotline or similar service or work in a genetics lab or with people with a genetic disease."

Certification and Licensing

The American Board of Genetic Counseling (ABGC) holds an examination every year for candidates seeking certification that shows they have studied and mastered the field of genetic counseling. Candidates must be graduates of a master's degree program from a school accredited by either the Accreditation Council for Genetic Counseling (ACGC) or the ABGC. The computer-based exam consists of two hundred questions, which must be answered within four hours. Those who pass the examination earn the title of certified genetic counselor.

Not all states require genetic counselors to have licenses, which gives the holder the right to practice genetic counseling

A genetic counselor discusses family medical history and genetic testing results with a patient. Genetic counselors help patients understand the risk of developing certain genetic diseases.

in a given jurisdiction. At the end of 2017, twenty-two states had formal licensing requirements, and the rest, with the exception of Wyoming and Vermont, were in the process of drawing up licensure rules and procedures. The requirements for a license vary by state; Indiana, for example, requires a transcript from a master's or doctoral program in genetic counseling, proof of ABGC exam certification, a criminal background check, and verification of any and all medical licenses held in any state.

Volunteer Work and Internships

For students interested in genetic counseling, volunteer opportunities offer experience in counseling others in good health and disease prevention. Suicide and distress hotlines, offering one-on-one counseling over the phone, teach the demands of working with individual patients. Hospitals, clinics, and hospices may offer positions in which volunteers spend time with disabled individuals, children, or terminally ill patients. Some schools have voluntary peer counselors who help students work through the stress of academics. A nonprofit pregnancy center may have volunteer positions for assistants who can gain experience in prenatal counseling.

Some genetic counselors allow shadowing, in which students or volunteers accompany them while they interpret test data and consult with patients. On its website, the National Society of Genetic Counselors offers a list of genetic counselors who invite contact from students. These counselors may give permission for a shadowing experience, either for a day or for several months.

An internship, paid or unpaid, can offer valuable work experience. Sanford Health in Sioux Falls, South Dakota, hires summer interns to help create pedigree drawings and enter patient data into an electronic medical records database. The Feinberg School of Medicine at Northwestern University in Chicago offers one-week summer internships. The program includes lectures, discussions, field trips, and contact with patients. Health research labs, including the Icahn School of Medicine at Mount Sinai in New York City and the National Cancer Institute outside Washington, DC, offer co-ops, in which students interrupt their studies for three to twelve months to work as a technician or assistant in a medical laboratory.

Skills and Personality

Genetic counselors need a strong interest in the life sciences, such as organic chemistry, biology, or medicine. Genetic counseling is a complex, fast-changing field that demands attention to current research. As new treatments become available, genetic counselors must clearly explain the science to patients who may not know the first thing about DNA mutations or inherited diseases.

A strong sense of empathy and patience are also required. Genetic counselors involve themselves in personal medical details as well as the dynamics of relationships and families. The results of a DNA test can make patients fearful and uncertain of their next steps. Careful listening and clear speaking on the part of a genetic counselor can guide them to treatment or explain other options if no treatment is available.

For many genetic counselors, the attraction of the job lies in the way it combines patient contact with cutting-edge science. "What genetic counseling gave me was a good split between patient care and the hard science research end of things," Megan McMinn told a CNBC.com interviewer. While studying biology at the University of Mount Union in Ohio, she had planned to become a physician's assistant but then took up genetic counseling. After seeing about six patients a day at a cancer clinic, she moved on to cardiology, assessing patients and their families for their genetic risk of heart disease.

On the Job

Employers

Most genetic counselors work in hospitals, but they may also be employed in a wide variety of clinical settings. A neurologist, for example, may hire a genetic counselor to counsel patients on their risk for inherited forms of epilepsy. Good Samaritan Hospital in Long Island, New York, offers prenatal and cancer genetic counseling. Some genetic counselors work in specialty clinics such as cancer treatment centers and cardiology centers, where genetic testing is offered alongside more traditional diagnostic tools such as echocardiograms, stress tests, and others.

Medical schools hire genetic counselors as teachers. Genetic counselors may also take part in medical research at a cancer foundation or a government agency such as the Office of Public Health Genomics at the Centers for Disease Control and Prevention in Atlanta. These settings promise the reward of new discoveries in a rapidly changing scientific field. They may also offer some contact with patients—the counseling part of this career that attracts many of its newcomers.

Working Conditions

Genetic counselors work indoors in a hospital, lab, or clinic. Most keep private offices and see patients there by appointment. A patient may call on his or her own or be referred to a genetic counselor by a family doctor. The main variable in the job is public contact. Whereas some genetic counselors see patients routinely, others are engaged in study or research that does not involve as much interaction with patients or test subjects.

Genetic counselors at the University of Oklahoma College of Medicine see cancer and heart patients referred to them by specialists. Using results from DNA tests, they can guide these patients on the possible genetic cause of their illness and their risk for other diseases. They also offer a genetic counseling clinic once a week. These clinics are one-hour consultations in which counselors go over test results and pedigrees with individuals and families.

Earnings

In 2016 the median salary for genetic counselors reached $74,120 per year, or $35.64 per hour, according to the Bureau of Labor Statistics (BLS). Genetic counselors in Maryland, Nevada, South Carolina, New Jersey, and Washington earned the highest mean wage in this occupation. Top employers for genetic counselors, according to the BLS, are hospitals (employing 900 as of 2016), physician offices (600), and laboratories (550). Outpatient care centers, which employed 140 genetic counselors, paid the highest annual mean wage: $84,720.

Opportunities for Advancement

Genetic counselors can move into executive positions in which they manage departments dedicated to testing, counseling, or research. If they prefer research or teaching, they can apply to a university department, a foundation, or a medical school faculty. Colleges, universities, and professional schools employed 250 genetic counselors as of 2016, according to BLS statistics. Genetic counselors can also bring their knowledge to commercial applications, such as the development of new testing kits for use by doctors or for sale to the public. And they can move geographically—the demand for their services is new and still developing in many countries.

What Is the Future Outlook for Genetic Counselors?

The demand for genetic counselors is growing. The BLS predicts a growth rate of 29 percent in positions open to genetic counselors through 2024. In large part, this growth stems from the many new discoveries in the genetics field, which give rise to testing methods with a much wider scope. The field of genetic counseling is growing more than four times faster than the average of 7 percent for all other occupations.

Genetic counselors can set up an individual or group practice, or they can cross medical specialties by working in a fertility clinic, advising couples hopeful for a healthy child. A cancer or heart clinic may need their services. Many hospitals are setting up new in-house genetic departments. This allows doctors and specialists on staff to work more closely with genetic counselors. They can avoid the delay of referring patients to outside counselors who work independently. Those interested in a career in genetic counseling should have no shortage of opportunities to work in the field in the coming years.

Find Out More

American Board of Genetic Counseling (ABGC)
4400 College Blvd., Suite 220
Overland Park, KS 66211
www.abgc.net

The ABGC certifies professional genetic counselors. The organization's website offers state-by-state licensing and certification guidelines.

Genetics Society of America (GSA)
9650 Rockville Pike
Bethesda, MD 20814
www.genetics-gsa.org

The GSA is a group of fifty-five hundred professional genetics researchers from more than fifty countries. The organization promotes research and education in the field, holds conferences, and publishes two scholarly journals: *Genetics* and *G3: Genes, Genomes, Genetics*.

National Society of Genetic Counselors (NSGC)
330 N. Wabash Ave., Suite 2000
Chicago, IL 60611
www.nsgc.org

Founded in 1979, the NSGC promotes the interests of genetic counselors in the health care industry. It provides a communications network, educational opportunities, and information on research through its publication, the *Journal of Genetic Counseling*. The website also offers assistance to people seeking genetic counseling via a patient resource site.

Biomedical Engineer

Biomedical Engineer

Minimum Educational Requirements
Bachelor's degree in biology, engineering, health sciences, or related field

Personal Qualities
Strong math and computer skills; problem-solving ability; knowledge of electrical and mechanical engineering

Certification and Licensing
Not required for biomedical engineers, although professional certification is possible through the Fundamentals of Engineering and Principles and Practice of Engineering exams

Working Conditions
Indoors in biomedical research labs and technology/engineering facilities

Salary Range
A median rate of $85,620 per year as of 2016

Number of Jobs
About 21,300 in 2016

Future Job Outlook
Average, with a growth rate of about 7 percent through 2026

What Does a Biomedical Engineer Do?

Biomedical engineers combine technology with health. They design artificial limbs, heart pacemakers, and other medical devices. Their engineering and design skills help disabled people and those with serious illnesses. Some biomedical engineers are designing artificial human organs. Others are involved with stem cell therapy, which can help repair damaged cells and organs. Some become experts in medical equipment and know how X-ray machines, baby incubators, and heart monitors work. They have the skills to repair and maintain these machines for the clinics, doctors, and hospitals that use them.

Biomedical engineers work in labs filled with high-tech equipment. There are lasers, microscopes, incubators, and cryogenic equipment for freezing human cells and tissue. Before starting work in a lab, a biomedical engineer goes through extensive training. There is a lot to know when dealing with advanced microscopes and cameras or when operating incubators, which are controlled spaces used to grow cells, examine microbes, or handle hazardous toxic materials. It is common for biomedical engineers to learn how to use cryogenic equipment, which is used for freezing cells, tissues, and organs. Many also learn how to operate medical lasers that carry out new noninvasive surgical procedures that do not involve scalpels, sutures, or loss of blood.

Laptop and desktop computers are also used in the work of a biomedical engineer. Computers with fast processing speeds and lots of memory are essential for designing prototypes of new equipment or for writing the software that runs this equipment. To understand how a machine will affect the human body, an engineer might also design a computer simulation or a clinical test on human or animal subjects.

Biomedical engineers need to think about safety because the job involves risks and dangers. A device that is implanted in the human body, for example, can cause serious, life-threatening infection. The body can also reject artificial organs or metal hips and knees designed in a lab. Testing equipment is a big part of the job, and a biomedical engineer might spend weeks at a time designing protocols, which are the instructions to be strictly followed in any lab or clinical trial.

The day-to-day job of biomedical engineering can involve writing reports, analyzing test results, and filling out applications. Having created an experimental device, a biomedical engineer might be involved with the long and complicated process of requesting approval of the device from the US Food and Drug Administration.

A research bioengineer, a type of biomedical engineer, works at the stages that come before testing or marketing of a biomedical product. The engineer may be doing work in electrical engineering and biology to understand how tiny circuits work at the level of individual cells. He or she may also be involved in perfecting a new artificial hand that works on nerve impulses received from the brain.

This work takes place at the frontiers of medical science. There are problems to solve, and there can be many false starts, detours, and delays. But there can also be multiple solutions to a single problem, all with their unique advantages. In an article posted on the Johns Hopkins Department of Biomedical Engineering website, Professor Warren Grayson explains, "Engineering is not like math where there is one right answer and many wrong answers. In engineering, there can be many right answers."

Another insight into this field is offered by Kam Leong, a bioengineer working at Columbia University in the field of nanotechnology—the science of designing microscopic medical therapies and devices. "Both biologists and engineers are problem solvers," Leong explains in an interview on the Columbia Systems Biology webpage. "But whereas biologists ask 'Why?' as an engineer I am trying to understand 'How?'"

With experience in the lab, bioengineers can move on to subspecialties within their field. One of these is biomaterials, which is the study of plastics, fibers, metal, and other materials that go into medical devices. Rehabilitative engineering concentrates on assistive devices and equipment to help patients recover from injuries or disease. And biomechanics is the study of natural biological systems, such as photosynthesis or cell division, for possible application to medical technology.

Some biomedical engineers specialize in diagnostic tools that help doctors discover illnesses. To create these devices, bioengineers use graphic design programs. They may work in teams, with individuals assigned to different parts of the device: materials, for instance, or the construction, instrumentation, or electronic circuitry. Others design and build next-generation devices, such as shock wave therapy machines, or improve traditional ones such as the old-fashioned sphygmomanometer, which measures blood pressure.

Systems-oriented biomedical engineers may work on software code. Computer programs test and run many new medical control devices and equipment, such as three-dimensional X-ray imagers, brain scan devices, and magnetic resonance imaging (MRI) machines. These machines process large amounts of data, which must be organized and presented in a logical way to the users.

Regardless of their specialty, biomedical engineers can make the once impossible happen and transform that impossibility into an everyday tool. One of the most famous breakthroughs in biological engineering, for example, is the system known as ACAT, or the assistive context-aware toolkit. Biomedical engineers trained the physicist Stephen Hawking, who was totally paralyzed by a progressive genetic disease, how to use ACAT to speak in real time through a digital speech synthesizer. Built on open source software, ACAT systems are now available to anyone with a computer.

How Do You Become a Biomedical Engineer?

Education

Students interested in biomedical engineering study human biology, physics, anatomy, and electrical and mechanical engineering. Additionally, it is important to study health services as a business sector. A biomedical engineer designing a robotic surgical instrument, for example, needs to know how that new product will meet a need in hospital operating rooms. Many universities offer a bachelor of science degree in biomedical engineering. At a minimum, employers generally require a four-year degree with a relevant major from applicants in this field.

For graduate students, many universities also offer fellowships—a short-term position in which the institution covers expenses for research and travel and offers concentrated training and experience in an area of interest to the applicant. Hospitals and medical centers also offer courses, degree programs, and research opportunities. The Mayo Clinic's biomedical engineering and physiology program, for example, hosts a clinic attended by more than one hundred doctoral candidates from all over the world. The program's researchers benefit from a direct link to the world's largest integrated medical services group.

Certification and Licensing

There is no licensing requirement for biomedical engineers, but employers may require clinical certification in engineering or certification as a biomedical equipment technician. For engineers, the National Council of Examiners for Engineering and Surveying administers two exams: the Fundamentals of Engineering and the Principles and Practice of Engineering. A candidate with a passing score for these two exams is awarded certification as a licensed professional engineer.

Internships and Volunteer Work

A paid or unpaid internship is a great way for students interested in biomedical engineering to get acquainted with new research in the field. Many private companies offer short internships to undergraduate students who already have some lab experience.

An internship in the public sector is another option. The National Institutes of Health (NIH), for example, offers the Biomedical Engineer Summer Internship Program for students who have completed their junior year in college. This ten-week program takes place at the NIH lab in Bethesda, Maryland, home to some of the world's top biomedical engineering scientists. Applications are reviewed in a national competition, with students selecting projects that interest them from a list provided by the NIH. For the sixteen interns selected for the 2017 program, projects included a microchip implant used for detecting HIV, a smartphone application that predicts car accidents on the basis of risky driving, and a Kinect keyboard, which works using hand and finger gestures, engineered for a wounded veteran.

Many nonprofit organizations and public health agencies welcome volunteers. This is a good way to meet patients and doctors who depend on biomedical devices. Biomedical engineering students who volunteer for a summer in a hospital's physical therapy department, for example, will get a close-up view of how prosthetic devices work—and where they fall short. Volunteer positions can also expose students to real-world issues, such as malnutrition and infectious disease, for which biomedical engineering may offer improvement to the lives and well-being of others.

Skills and Personality

Biomedical engineers need math skills, engineering knowledge, and problem-solving ability. Attention to detail is necessary when working with or designing complex, expensive medical equipment. They must be able to clearly discuss complex scientific concepts with patients and other engineers and enjoy working with a team of colleagues. The hours can be long, and the work demands intelligence, patience, and empathy for the needs of doctors and patients.

Employers

Many biomedical engineers are employed by research institutes, some of which are affiliated with large universities. Private companies such as Medtronic and St. Jude Medical also employ large engineering staffs. The NIH, a federal agency, includes the National Institute of Biomedical Imaging and Bioengineering. The institute was founded in 2000 and is now the largest source of funding for biomedical engineering in the world. Biomedical engineers also work for large hospitals and medical centers.

Working Conditions

Some biomedical engineers work in research lab settings, and others spend their days in hospitals and clinics, assisting with biomedical devices used by patients. Companies that manufacture the instruments may have engineers involved in the production setting, ensuring that the devices meet quality control standards. It is common for biomedical engineers to use computers, measuring devices, and complex testing equipment while developing new products or processes.

Earnings

The Bureau of Labor Statistics (BLS) calculated the median pay for biomedical engineers in 2016 as $85,620 a year, or $41.16 an hour. The highest salaries in the ninetieth percentile of biomedical engineers began at $134,620 a year. Salary levels average highest in research and development (R&D) departments that depend on engineering skills and life sciences knowledge. At the next salary level are engineers creating medical, measuring, and navigational and control equipment, areas in which R&D breakthroughs are applied in the development of new products. Health care and educational settings fall on the low end of the pay scale.

Opportunities for Advancement

With experience, biomedical engineers can seek out new opportunities as supervisors and department managers. Rising into these ranks may bring a chance to apply for the post of director, an individual who decides on the types of research and products an institution will develop. There are also academic positions, including professorships, open to biomedical engineers with a deep knowledge of the field and a successful track record. Tenured academic positions hold the opportunity for independent research, an excellent salary, and long-term job security.

What Is the Future Outlook for Biomedical Engineers?

The BLS predicts jobs for biomedical engineers will grow at a rate of 7 percent through 2026. In this innovative field, the demand for new workers is driven by the constant development of new medical devices and processes and the improvement of others, such as prosthetics, that have been available for decades. Competition is keen for talent among biomedical companies, as a successful commercial application can mean enormous revenues and profits. Research labs also need skilled biomedical engineers who can bring their knowledge of other technologies, such as quantum computing and three-dimensional printing, to the field.

Find Out More

Biomedical Engineering Society (BMES)
8201 Corporate Dr., Suite 1125
Landover, MD 20785
www.bmes.org

A professional home for biomedical engineers, the BMES holds an annual meeting offering more than two thousand scientific presentations as well as a career fair, exhibit hall, and career development sessions. A searchable directory on the group's website allows students interested in the field to find biomedical engineering mentors, special interest groups, and online education courses.

BioMediKal.In
http://biomedikal.in

This website, created by Indian biomedical engineering student Kush Tripathi, offers information on the field in India and across the globe. The site features articles and videos on technical breakthroughs, current research, and new bioengineering applications, such as the use of cells taken from the umbilical cord to treat heart disease.

Engineering in Medicine and Biology Society
445 Hoes Ln.
Piscataway, NJ 08854
www.embs.org

This international society of biomedical engineers has members in ninety-seven countries. Local chapters and clubs welcome professionals as well as students, who can network, attend a workshop or lecture, or present original research. The website features a job board and news from technical committees focusing on signal processing, wearable sensors, biorobotics, and other specialties.

Johns Hopkins Department of Biomedical Engineering
720 Rutland Ave.
Baltimore, MD 21205
www.bme.jhu.edu

Johns Hopkins has one of the nation's top biomedical engineering departments. The department's Center for Bioengineering Innovation and Design offers an annual Healthcare Innovation Showcase in which a panel of industry experts share their advice on bringing new technology to the commercial market. In addition, the department's website features current student projects and research.

Biological Technician

Biological Technician

Minimum Educational Requirements
Bachelor's degree in biology, chemistry, or related scientific field; some jobs require only a certificate course in lab technology

Personal Qualities
Patience; attention to detail; ability to multitask and work under pressure; good communication skills

Certification and Licensing
Not required by state licensing boards; some employers may request certification as a medical laboratory technician or medical laboratory scientist

Working Conditions
Regular daytime hours working with a team of colleagues in indoor research laboratories, clinic and hospital offices, and commercial testing facilities

Salary Range
From $27,660 to $69,550 per year, with median annual pay falling at $42,520 as of 2016

Number of Jobs
About 82,100 as of 2016

Future Job Outlook
Faster-than-average job growth of 10 percent through 2026

What Does a Biological Technician Do?

Biological technicians (or biotechs) work in laboratories gathering data needed by doctors, scientists, and researchers. To gather data, they use basic lab equipment such as microscopes and scales as well as more advanced gear: centrifuges, evaporators, and the all-important autoclaves, which are used to sterilize equipment. It is common for biological technicians to measure results, take observations, enter the numbers into a database, and write reports on their observations and test outcomes.

Some biotechs work under the management of scientists who design research work or clinical trials and supervise the test environment. Many others work for hospitals and clinics where they carry out tests ordered by doctors to measure the health of patients.

In an interview with DrKit.org, Bonita, a trainee at the clinical science lab course at the University of West Florida, explains the role of a biotech: "When the doctor orders [a lab test], we're the ones that run it first, and we give the diagnosis. We can't actually give it to the person or the patient, but we're the ones that run the test and perform it to show the doctor exactly what they're looking for."

In the course of a day, many biotechs work with soil or blood samples or with live animals serving as test subjects. Some analyze tissue samples and test whether a tumor is benign or cancerous. Others may work in human drug trials; these tests measure the safety and effectiveness of new medications. Some biotechs test crops or food destined for grocery shelves.

Many companies that require drug screens call on commercial test labs to do the work. A biological technician would be responsible for collecting a urine sample, carrying out the test, and filing the result form with the employer. The same kind of work takes place in hospitals, sometimes under emergency conditions. A new patient who has overdosed and is unconscious must be tested—fast. While the emergency room doctor makes observations and nurses take the patient's pulse and blood pressure, the tech breaks out a small kit known as an assay that will, hopefully, reveal the drug responsible for the overdose.

Biotechs work in teams, and many work in an academic setting, which can pose its unique challenges. Sophie Hill, a lab technician at the University of Birmingham, comments in a YouTube interview on one particular challenge: "A bad day would be when we have four practicals [projects] starting at the same time, and everybody's running around trying to get everything done, and you've got 500 students in the way."

A big part of the job, no matter the setting, is maintaining equipment and the work areas in the lab. Safety and cleanliness are vital in medical laboratories. The techs have to keep their lab benches clean and their gear, such as skin sensors and syringes, sterile to protect patients or research subjects.

With experience, a biological technician can gain new responsibilities. Researchers may call on a technician to help design a new drug trial. This means drawing up protocols; these are the guidelines for how many subjects will be tested and how the test will be carried out. The tech may also set up a schedule, interview and enroll volunteers, administer the drug, observe any side effects, and present the data and results of the trial in a summary.

Although biological technicians usually work in clean labs, environmental testing may bring them outdoors. A county that requests testing of its wetlands for toxic chemicals, for example, will call on labs and techs with the needed equipment and experience. The tech carries out the work to measure any environmental damage, sometimes under hazardous conditions. Biotechs are needed to clean oil-soaked birds when a tanker or drilling rig has a spill. They may also travel abroad to war or epidemic zones to carry out tests, perform routine patient care, and save lives.

Biological technicians are also needed to examine blood and DNA samples in crime labs. They examine animals for the presence of diseases that threaten the food supply. They show up unannounced at greenhouses, stockyards, and fish hatcheries to ensure these areas meet public health standards. In any setting, they are responsible for gathering data and keeping it stored and organized.

How Do You Become a Biological Technician?

Education

To enter this field, applicants need a bachelor's degree in biology, chemistry, or a related scientific field as well as some experience in a school or commercial laboratory. A transcript showing courses in genetics, environmental science, or physiology is also helpful, as are basic courses in math, health science, and physics.

For some positions, employers may accept an associate's degree, which takes two years of course work. Biological technicians also need to demonstrate an ability to handle computers. They need computer skills to record, store, and transmit data; to write reports; and to analyze samples.

Many colleges offer a step up and into the field through clinical science lab courses in which students train in the everyday tasks of a working medical lab. "Everything that we do in the lab is directly correlated to what we're going to be doing in the hospital," explains Bonita of the University of West Florida's clinical lab program. "It's the same exact test, we have the same exact instruments, and the same exact paperwork."

Certification and Licensing

Biological technicians do not need a state license. To show knowledge and competence in their field, however, they must pass exams to become certified as medical laboratory technicians or medical science technicians. Various organizations offer exams and issue certificates, setting their own requirements for candidates. The American Association of Bioanalysts, for example, offers a medical technician certificate to those who pass a basic knowledge exam. To apply, a candidate needs at least an associate's degree with a major in laboratory science or medical technology.

Internships and Volunteer Work

Hospitals, research labs, and private companies offer internships that prepare future biological technicians for the demands of this career. Lab interns may carry out the basic tasks of taking samples, running testing equipment, or interviewing patients and test subjects. Environmental groups accept volunteers to monitor invasive species, test water samples, or survey wildlife habitat. Some groups working in remote areas provide interns with housing and a basic living allowance.

Drug companies carrying out drug trials, which involve a lot of data entry and paperwork, often employ interns. A temporary internship can lead to a permanent job offer. It can also teach vital skills to a lab technician: how to safely handle samples, how to administer drugs under review to test subjects, and how to process aliquot samples—a method of dividing a solution into precisely equal portions.

Skills and Personality

Biological technicians should have a strong interest in math and science. They must be comfortable with the daily use and maintenance of testing and measuring equipment. Work in a laboratory setting demands attention to detail, the ability to follow instructions, written and oral communication skills, and precision with numbers, observations, and calculations. Critical-thinking skills and the ability to reason are important in tech jobs with more responsibility or those that involve analyzing test data and designing research experiments. Because biological technicians are often called on to troubleshoot temperamental devices, some aptitude for the maintenance and repair of complex equipment is also useful.

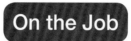
On the Job

Employers
Most biological technicians work for scientific or medical labs operated by hospitals, research institutes, public health agencies, or private companies involved in the biosciences. Others may work in the outdoors, collecting samples and carrying out research for environmental biologists, food companies, or zoologists. Drug companies need technicians to staff their testing and research laboratories. Larger companies need biological technicians to monitor the health and safety of their workers or to measure the environmental impact of their production processes.

Working Conditions
Most biological technicians work indoors in a laboratory setting. They work with a team of colleagues under the supervision of a head scientist or, in a medical setting, a lab supervisor. The work can be dangerous. Some techs handle dangerous organisms such as viruses and bacteria. They also come in contact with tissue, blood, and various other bodily fluids that can transmit disease.

Additionally, the work can be physically tough. There can be a lot of standing, lifting, and hurried moving around in a crowded bio lab, and biological technicians working outdoors may deal with bad weather and rugged terrain. And it can be noisy: medical testing equipment generates a constant stream of sound as well as high-pitched electronic signals and alarms.

Earnings
The median salary for biological technicians reached $42,520 in 2016. Average salaries vary with specific fields and sectors. In the pharmaceutical industry, for example, the median wage for this occupation was $46,610 in 2016, and biological technicians

working in the federal government reached a median salary of $36,020. Hospitals, both public and private, fell in the middle of this range, paying a median of $41,530 annually to their biotechs.

Opportunities for Advancement

With lab experience and an advanced degree, a biological technician can move into the ranks of research scientists. A biotech may also take on the role of lab supervisor or manager, or he or she may move into the education sector as an instructor or adviser. At a hospital or pharmaceutical company, the deep knowledge of testing and lab procedures that a biological technician develops over time enhances the chances for promotion into management. An interest in engineering or manufacturing may also bring new opportunities with greater responsibilities in the medical device business.

What Is the Future Outlook for Biological Technicians?

The demand for biological technicians runs high across many different fields and employers. The demand for medical services in the United States is strong and increasing, meaning skilled technicians will be needed in hospitals, clinics, walk-in medical centers, and doctor's offices. Research labs are exploring new methods of healing and illness prevention, and biotechs will be needed to assist in their work: studying inherited illnesses, slowing the aging process, and creating artificial tissue, limbs, and organs. Environmental technicians will be called on to research new methods of combating pollution, developing biofuels and other new energy sources, and ensuring the safety of the food supply. Scientists working on the new frontier in biology—cloning and synthetic organisms—will need biological technicians to assist in their experiments and bring their new products to market.

Find Out More

All Allied Health Schools
www.allalliedhealthschools.com

31

This website's "Medical Technician Education and Career Guide" is a valuable source for information on technician training. The guide covers degree programs, qualifying exams, certification, and schools, as well as provides detailed descriptions and requirements for the many different jobs in this wide-ranging field.

American Institute of Biological Sciences (AIBS)
1313 Dolley Madison Blvd., Suite 402
McLean, VA 22101
www.aibs.org

The AIBS provides peer review and support services to biology research projects and creates community programs that promote the profession of research biology. Its website offers links to job-hunting sites and research experiences for undergraduates. The institute also produces the *BioScience Talks* podcast series.

American Medical Technologists (AMT)
10700 W. Higgins Rd., Suite 150
Rosemont, IL 60018
www.americanmedtech.org

The AMT is a resource for technicians seeking certification. To advance in their careers, lab technicians can prepare for and pass AMT certification exams that demonstrate their proficiency at current medical lab practices. The website provides study resources, applications, and exam schedules, as well as education requirements, a salary guide, and some professional profiles.

Federation of American Societies for Experimental Biology (FASEB) Career Center
https://careers.faseb.org

A source for employers and jobseekers, FASEB claims to be the largest source of biology jobs in the nation. Its Career Center offers jobs in various specialties and settings, from university research labs to pharmaceutical companies, environmental research groups, health care, and public disease control. The site also features a free résumé review.

Microbiologist

What Does a Microbiologist Do?

There is an invisible world of tiny organisms living around and within us. This micro world of bacteria, viruses, fungi, and other parasites has a mega impact on human health and well-being. It is the job of a microbiologist to study these organisms and develop new ways of controlling and harnessing them to society's benefit.

Microbiologists work in laboratories using microscopes and other high-tech equipment to carry out their research. They do not work alone—most microbiologists join large teams made up of specialists, assistants, technicians, and supervisors. Their hours can be long, but their job duties and schedules vary. Interviewed by the website Science-Buddies, microbiologist Mary Birtnick describes her usual tasks of the day: "Every day is different. A typical day starts between 8 and 9 a.m. and ends between 6 and 8 p.m. I spend my time designing and carrying out experiments, keeping up to date with the current microbiology literature, meeting with colleagues, writing manuscripts and grant applications, as well as participating in teaching microbiology classes."

A major part of the job is simply keeping up with the stream of data and information in a constantly changing field. Microbiologists publish their findings in research papers and in articles appearing in scientific and medical journals. Staying current means reading scientific literature, attending conferences and seminars, and going to lectures. A big part of a microbiologist's job may be communicating with the public, an urgent task in the case of a disease outbreak or epidemic.

There are various specialties in which microbiologists work. Medical microbiologists work in the health field. They study pathogens, the microorganisms that cause serious, sometimes deadly diseases such as influenza, meningitis, or Ebola. Using samples taken from ill patients, they assist medical doctors in diagnosis and treatment. What interests microbiologists is the effect of a pathogen and how it moves from one person to another. They work to cure the sick and prevent disease from spreading.

For a pharmaceutical company, a microbiologist might help develop a new drug to combat an infectious disease. To carry out this work, the microbiologist would have to analyze a strain of bacteria or virus to develop a way to neutralize the organism, destroy it outright, or interfere with its ability to reproduce. A microbiologist may also be able to boost the body's natural defenses against the organism via a new drug.

Other specialists in the field call themselves bacteriologists, parasitologists, or mycologists (those who study fungi, such as mushrooms). Pathologists study pathogenic disease, and immunologists are experts in the immune systems of humans and animals. Some microbiologists combine these specialties and work outside the research lab. Environmental microbiologists take to the outdoors to collect and study samples of microbes in air, water, soil, and animals.

Virologists specialize in viruses. These are tiny organisms made up of a coating of protein and a genetic code transmitted by DNA or RNA. A virologist seeks to prevent the spread of viral illnesses such as hepatitis, measles, or chicken pox. It is a never-ending battle, as many viruses can evolve to resist medicines created to kill them off. Research virologists are on the front lines, developing new ways to prevent viruses from replicating themselves in even more dangerous forms.

A virologist can spend his or her career fighting a single disease by tracing outbreaks, testing patients, and developing new vaccines. The virologist Jonas Salk is famous the world over for his work on the polio vaccine during the 1940s and 1950s. In this century, thousands of microbiologists are focusing their work on hepatitis and HIV/AIDS.

No matter the specialty, an important part of a microbiologist's job is to analyze specimens of blood, tissue, and organs for the presence of microbes. The standard tool for this work is the electron microscope, which can magnify an image up to 10 million times. Microbiologists also learn to use a wide variety of testing kits and portable labs, which are expensive, complex tools used to discover pathogens in food or water.

Conducting validation tests is another common part of a microbiologist's job. These are meant to ensure that tests and medications are safely and effectively doing what they are designed to do. Without validation tests, hospitals may not be detecting dangerous flu strains, or a drug company's products may be interacting with other drugs in a way that endangers patients.

Microbiologists need to have some basic skills. One of these is preparing culture media, which are small plastic dishes with organic substances that are designed to keep microorganisms alive and nourished. This task is a bit like cooking—the first step is to assemble the tools and ingredients, after which there are steps in mixing, heating, and sterilization.

To carry out this work, microbiologists use measuring cylinders, flasks, lab scales, chemical spoons, test tubes, pH meters that measure acidity, dispensers, and incubators. Precautions must be taken—a microbiologist's lab can be a dangerous place. They often handle solvents and even hazardous chemicals that can cause fires or acids and bases that can burn flesh.

Microbiologists must have a talent for keeping research laboratories clean, safe, and sterile. When working with very small organisms, any dust, mold, or germs in the air or on surfaces can contaminate samples and render test results worthless. Samples have to be labeled, stored, and kept under the right conditions, and their movement across the lab must be tracked in a secure database. Humidity and temperature, as well as light intensity, are carefully controlled in all storage areas. Microbiologists also must follow very strict protocols about keeping their skin, hair, and clothing as clean as possible.

With experience, microbiologists can move into more dangerous and tightly secured labs. These facilities go by a scale of biosafety levels (BSL) from BSL-1 to BSL-4, with the latter used for the most dangerous disease microbes that can be transmitted through the air or for which there is no vaccine. At the BSL-4 level, entrance and movement is strictly controlled, and workers use airlocks, decontamination chambers, biosafety cabinets, and protective suits and hoods.

How Do You Become a Microbiologist?

Education

Preparation for a career in microbiology begins at the high school level with courses in biology, chemistry, physics, math, and computer science. English and/or communication courses train future scientists for their work on journal articles, scientific papers, and speeches. Participation in science fairs and extracurricular labs and clubs, if available, also lends a future microbiologist valuable experience.

Microbiologists applying for a lab position need at least a bachelor's degree with a major in a relevant field of study. More than two hundred US universities offer four-year degrees in microbiology. Courses in math and statistics are also useful in this field, which often involves the analysis of complex data. Related majors include biochemistry, medical laboratory sciences, physiology, and molecular and cell biology. Some exploration in immunology, virology, pathology, and parasitology will help direct a college-level student to an interesting specialization.

A microbiologist studies organisms that affect human health. Their work is used to develop new medicines, to help diagnose and treat illnesses, to track down the source of diseases, and for other similar purposes.

Laboratory experience is vital for future professional microbiologists. For those hoping to carry out independent research at the university level or at a private institute, a doctorate is usually required. Jobs supervising a microbiology lab will often require a doctorate, as well as prior experience in a management role.

Certification and Licensing

Microbiologists need state licensing in certain circumstances. A license requirement, for example, is common for microbiologists working in public health departments or food safety labs and for clinical microbiologists working in the health care field. In California, for example, an employer may require a certified clinical laboratory microbiologist scientist license. The state Health and Human Services Agency issues these licenses after an applicant passes a test on California lab laws and regulations. Also required is a bachelor's degree and at least one year of postgraduate work or training.

Internships and Volunteer Work

Internships offer experience in laboratory work and applied research—that is, research used to solve a specific real-world problem. If the position is paid, the salary may be set on a sliding scale according to the applicant's academic level. To meet health and safety standards, employers may also require some prior lab experience.

Internships often involve technical support for research teams in the lab or assistance with sample collection in a public or natural setting. They may involve keeping records, preserving samples, analyzing samples, maintaining facilities and equipment—all basic tasks crucial to the management of a science lab. Internships also offer exposure to current research in a field of interest to the student, such as cancer, viral disease, or women's health.

Volunteer work can take microbiologists abroad to support disease research, environmental projects, green energy development, or the work of medical teams. This firsthand experience can broaden and deepen the knowledge gained in a science classroom. Spending time in a volunteer position also shows future employers that the microbiologist is willing to donate his or her own time and work to gain experience in the field.

Skills and Personality

To carry out precise analyses of test and experiment results, microbiologists need attention to detail, patience, record-keeping ability, and the talent to think through science problems logically. They need communication and writing skills as their work requires the clear reporting of research and test findings. The ability to manage work and time efficiently is also key for meeting project and research deadlines.

On the Job

Employers

Microbiologists are hired by state and city health departments, by hospitals, and by the federal government. Public agencies play a vital role in informing the public about disease threats, ranging from seasonal flu epidemics to outbreaks of tuberculosis and the bubonic plague. They may assign a newly hired microbiologist to a specific project, such as the study of the growing resistance among pathogens to antibiotic drugs.

Pharmaceutical companies hire microbiologists to research diseases and develop new drugs. At the university level, microbiologists teach their discipline and related subjects such as cell biology, organic chemistry, and virology. Hospitals and medical clinics also need microbiologists to help in the diagnosis and treatment of illnesses.

Working Conditions

Microbiologists work in laboratories, in classrooms, and in the field. The lab setting provides an environment for research and experiments, with technicians assisting with the equipment and supervisors guiding the work schedule. Out of the lab, microbiologists conduct onsite visits to guard against health hazards and collect samples from outdoor settings to investigate the source of disease outbreaks. For research institutes, the job may also require some public speaking. Microbiologists are often called on to explain their work to the public, at scientific conferences, or at meetings of investors.

Earnings

Microbiologists earned a median wage of $66,850 in 2016. Salaries vary widely, with the Bureau of Labor Statistics reporting a range of $39,480 to $128,190 in 2016. The highest median wages in that year were paid by the federal government ($101,320) and the lowest were in the education sector ($49,300). Pharmaceutical companies and state governments fall in the middle of the salary range.

Opportunities for Advancement

With experience, microbiologists can move into positions of greater responsibility. They can become laboratory directors or research project managers. A microbiologist may be promoted to head up a research and development department or win appointment as the head of a public health agency. Those seeking the freedom to do their own independent research may have the chance to organize and run their own labs, with responsibility for securing funding and setting goals and deadlines for their teams. Microbiologists with knowledge of related fields such as environmental science will have the best chances to secure better-paying, interesting jobs.

What Is the Future Outlook for Microbiologists?

Microbiology is an essential field of science, one relevant to medicine, drug research, public health, and important commercial sectors such as food production. Robots cannot do microbiology research—it takes the creative human mind to develop new approaches to problems such as cancer treatment. Jobs in the field are expected to increase, especially with breakthroughs in the search for new, cleaner sources of energy, such as biofuels, in pollution control (in which new microbes are "eating" air and water pollutants), and in genetically engineered crops.

Find Out More

About Bioscience: Bioscience Careers, "Microbiologist"
www.aboutbioscience.org/careers/microbiologist

This page describes the work of microbiologists in various settings, including research laboratories, the food industry, hospital/clinical laboratories, and education.

American Society for Microbiology (ASM)
1752 N St. NW
Washington, DC 20036
www.asmcareerconnections.org

The ASM is the leading professional society for microbiologists. On its Career Connections page, the group gathers a wealth of information for those seeking to launch their careers in the field, including a searchable database of job listings, résumé and interview guides, networking resources, and one-on-one coaching from a career strategist.

Microbiology Society

12 Roger St.
London WC1N 2JU
England
https://microbiologysociety.org/

Based in London, this group has a worldwide membership drawn from universities, industry, hospitals, and research institutes. The Careers section has advice on different non-research job paths—in education, media, law, and business—that a trained microbiologist can follow.

Nature

www.nature.com

This prestigious scientific journal posts links to its articles by subject, including microbiology. The articles offer a window into the latest research in the field. The microbiology page also serves as a go-to information source for scientists whenever a new disease epidemic develops.

Food Scientist

At a Glance

Food Scientist

Minimum Educational Requirements
Bachelor's degree; best majors are biology, chemistry, physics, or agricultural science

Personal Qualities
Curiosity; attention to detail; problem-solving ability; interest in health sciences and nutrition

Certification and Licensing
Only needed for certain jobs, such as public food inspector or health inspector; certification as a certified food scientist is the standard professional credential

Working Conditions
Indoors in research and testing laboratories and in the field working with food producers, processors, and commercial food companies

Salary Range
Median pay of $62,920 per year, or $30.25 an hour, as of 2016

Number of Jobs
43,000 through 2016

Future Job Outlook
Average growth rate of 7 percent through 2026

What Does a Food Scientist Do?

When Jorge Heraud was a boy, he spent summers with his grandparents, who grew tomatoes and rice on their farm in Peru. He was a city boy, fascinated by math and machinery. He did not think much about where his food came from, but those summers in the country made him realize that a big part of farming was hard, boring physical work. "There'd be dozens of us kids in the fields bending and picking, bending and picking weeds," he told *Bloomberg Businessweek*. "I must have been 7 when I first thought, 'This is a job for machines.'"

Heraud now lives and works in California, where his start-up company, Blue River Technology, builds robotic weedkillers that target weeds with microbursts of herbicide. Instead of spraying an entire field of soil and crops with weedkiller, the bots allow farmers to use less chemicals, helping to keep soil and plants largely free of dangerous toxins. These bots represent the next generation of food technology, designed to lessen the impact of chemicals on the soil and plants.

An interest and background in farming is a common trait among food scientists. A food scientist is like a farmer moving into a scientific laboratory and working with high-tech equipment rather than heavy machinery. But unlike farmers, food scientists hold regular hours, do not have to get up so early, and usually do not get their hands dirty.

Heraud and other food scientists are experts in food along the entire supply chain, from the farmer's field to the dinner table. Their basic job is to ensure the safety of food growing, packaging, storage, and shipment. Plant scientists work with crop growers to improve crop yields and quality. A key part of this work is research into new and improved strains of important food crops such as corn, wheat, and soybeans, using genetically modified organisms. These new strains are designed to deliver better yields as well as disease- and pest-resistant crops.

Food scientists also work with livestock farmers to study the nutrition, growth, and development of animals raised for food. They may recommend better housing, immunization, or feed to enhance the health and well-being of livestock destined for the commercial food market. As a result of the work of food scientists, grocery stores now stock cage-free eggs, grass-fed beef, and wild-caught fish. One of the latest products coming out of this work is A2 milk, which lacks a protein that causes digestive problems for humans.

Working in private companies, food scientists spend much of their time analyzing food, using a variety of testing and lab equipment. They take samples and test for microbes and pathogens. They study nutritional components of food, measuring those components for the labeling that goes on nearly every product made in the United States for human consumption. They may also work in the public sector to enforce health and safety regulations governing the shipment, processing, and storage of food.

Some food scientists work in universities and research institutes. Many are working on grants from the government and private companies to study the nation's food supply and production. With experience, they may be given responsibility over a laboratory or food science department or may be called on to lecture students on the subject. An important part of a research job is seeking out and applying for these grants, which demand good oral and written communication skills as well as the ability to assemble teams to carry out the research when the funding arrives.

Food scientists work to keep the food supply safe from harmful microbes. They are constantly testing food samples for the presence of salmonella, E. coli, listeria, and other pathogens that can harm consumers. They are experts in food poisoning and food spoilage, caused by the many different varieties of yeasts and molds. They know about safe food transport and packaging; they know how to measure the shelf life of a product and set food expiration dates. Many work for food companies that do not want their products appearing on the news for making people sick. Some work for government entities, such as the US Food and Drug Administration (FDA), a federal agency that enforces food safety standards.

When a foodborne illness breaks out, food scientists become emergency responders. They are called to investigate the nature of the illness and find the source. The work takes place under pressure, with government officials and the public demanding answers and money on the line for the producer of the contaminated food. The source of the illness may be a restaurant, grocery store, or food production facility. The food may have been prepared in unsanitary conditions or may have come into contact with an ill worker or consumer.

The public demand for safe food free of chemical preservatives also leads food scientists on the search for natural substitutes. Food scientists working for nonprofit agencies may travel to countries experiencing malnutrition and food shortages. They work to improve the distribution of food to these areas while also helping farmers achieve more disease- and drought-resistant strains and better yields.

How Do You Become a Food Scientist?

Education

For a career as a food scientist, students prepare with courses in biology, chemistry, engineering, plant biology, botany, nutrition, and environmental science. Also helpful are agricultural science courses in the areas of soil and plant chemistry, animal husbandry, crop science, and agricultural engineering. Some knowledge of health sciences and lab experience also will prepare students for the job market. Many food scientists moved into the field after an undergraduate course in culinary science, for which many community colleges and vocational-technical schools offer two- or three-year programs.

A bachelor's degree prepares students to apply for entry-level jobs. A master's degree or doctorate is valuable on an application for a research scientist job, as are advanced degrees in toxicology, plant genetics, and biotechnology. These degrees also allow food scientists to move into areas of specialization, such as foodborne illnesses, production engineering, plant or animal genetics, and statistics.

Certification and Licensing

There are many jobs related to food science, with some of them requiring a state or local license. A licensed health inspector for a city, for example, may be involved in screening restaurants and grocery stores for conditions of their food supply and storage. A state may also require licensing or registration for nutritionists and dieticians.

The Institute of Food Technologists (IFT) issues a credential for a certified food scientist (CFS). To attain it, applicants must already have a degree and some work experience. The amount of work experience required depends on the degree: those who hold a bachelor's degree in food science, for example, must have three years of full-time work experience, and those with a degree in a related field must have six.

After applying for the CFS, candidates must pass a three-hour exam consisting of 120 questions. The IFT requires that CFS holders earn seventy-five continuing education units (CEUs) over five years to maintain the certification. A CEU is earned by attending a qualified course or lecture on food science or a related field.

Internships and Volunteer Work

Many companies in the food business offer full- or part-time summer internships. These positions bring students face-to-face with a multibillion-dollar industry and how it prepares, packages, and markets its products. An intern may assist in the operations of a test kitchen, work with a product development team, or take part in a marketing department's consumer surveys. Most internships require some preparatory coursework in fields such as nutrition, culinary science, or plant biology.

Volunteering is another option that expands the contacts and networks that are essential to jobseekers. Sponsors include public health departments and food banks that offer meals to the needy. Nonprofits, such as the Partnership for Food Safety Education, also accept volunteers to assist in informing the public about food safety and the dangers of foodborne illnesses.

Skills and Personality

A food scientist needs to be very detail oriented. Measuring and testing in any field related to public health—such as food production—requires care and precision. An ability to work as part of a team and good communication skills are also useful, as is a talent for understanding and solving complex scientific problems. Also very useful to a food scientist is a sense of curiosity about food production at the source: farms, ranches, orchards, fish ponds, and greenhouses.

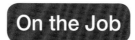

On the Job

Employers

For the purpose of ensuring a safe food supply, public health agencies need food scientists, as do federal agencies such as the FDA. Commercial food companies hire scientists to carry out testing and research and to develop recipes and formulas for new products. Food scientists also work for large agricultural commodity companies, such as Cargill and Archer Daniels Midland, to improve seed strains, develop new methods of animal husbandry, and research the growing, harvesting, packaging, and shipping of food crops. Nonprofits engage food scientists to improve farming and food supply conditions in developing countries and to help prevent the spread of foodborne illnesses.

A food scientist is like a farmer moving into a scientific laboratory and working with high-tech equipment rather than heavy machinery. But unlike farmers, food scientists hold regular hours, do not have to get up so early, and usually do not get their hands dirty.

Working Conditions

Many food scientists work in research and testing labs. They may also work in commercial production facilities, where they test and inspect heavy machinery, refrigeration equipment, and storage areas. Typically, they work with partners as part of a team—this is not a career for those who enjoy working alone or independently. Some food scientists travel to farms and other production facilities to carry out their investigations.

Earnings

Median pay for food scientists reached $62,920 in 2016, with a range from $37,660 to $116,520. Median annual pay ranged from $52,170 for food scientists teaching at colleges, universities, and professional schools to $76,050 for those employed in research and development departments. As with other jobs, those holding advanced degrees earn, on average, more than those holding bachelor's or associate's degrees.

Opportunities for Advancement

With experience and training, food scientists can move into positions with more responsibility, such as head researcher or lab director, or into management of a public health department. Many skills in this sector translate across employers. A food scientist familiar with food pathogens, for example, can move from a commercial food testing lab to a teaching position or become an inspector for the FDA. The need for creative solutions to food and water shortages and the spread of foodborne illness means a food scientist may find his or her skills in demand by private-sector employers, from start-up companies to large multinationals that serve a global market.

What Is the Future Outlook for Food Scientists?

The Bureau of Labor Statistics projects the job market for food scientists to grow at a 7 percent pace through the year 2026. This is a big and complex field with relevance to many sectors of the economy, from agriculture to food retailing, health care, hotels and restaurants, and marketing. New developments in food production methods, such as the use of genetically modified organisms, mean more scientists engaged in research. Food scientists will also be in demand to research plant disease, water supply and quality, biofuels, and the effects of climate change on farmers.

As a growing population puts more stress on available resources, the demand will rise for food scientists who can find solutions for a dependable global food supply. There will even be researchers developing food for astronauts, space tourists, and future colonists on Mars. There are few things as vital to humans as diet and food, meaning the importance of food science will remain high in decades to come.

Find Out More

Food and Agriculture Organization of the United Nations
www.fao.org/about/en

This global nonprofit focuses on antihunger programs and projects. Its website has a wealth of reports and data on the world's food supply system and a country-by-country rundown of the global state of nutrition and food availability.

Institute of Food Technologists
525 W. Van Buren St., Suite 1000
Chicago, IL 60607
www.ift.org

This is a global organization dedicated to providing a safe, nutritious, and sustainable food supply to countries around the world. Its website features the latest news on the food technology front. A Career Center page lists jobs as well as volunteer and mentoring opportunities.

Opus International
1191 E. Newport Center Dr., Suite PH-E
Deerfield Beach, FL 33442
www.foodscience.com

This company bills itself as an "executive recruiter to the food science industry." Its website lists open jobs as well as job-hunting tips, student internships, and contact information for various experts in the field. The site also includes a list of the companies that hire food scientists.

Texas A&M University Department of Nutrition and Food Science
https://nfs.tamu.edu

The department's Careers in Food Science and Technology web page gives information on the different food services jobs in the areas of food inspection, research and development, education, and sales. It also provides information on the major public-sector employers of food scientists, from the federal level down to the city level, concentrating on Texas.

Gene Therapy Researcher

At a Glance

Gene Therapy Researcher

Minimum Educational Requirements
Master's degree, with a concentration in genetics, cellular or molecular biology, immunology, or virology

Personal Qualities
Interest in health sciences and genetic disorders; problem-solving ability; skill with digital systems and large, complex databases

Certification and Licensing
Not required, except for medical licenses required of gene therapy researchers who carry out clinical trials of medications or procedures on patients

Working Conditions
In medical laboratories working with dedicated teams of researchers, technicians, and supervisors

Salary Range
A range of $42,040 to $116,680 and a median pay of $74,790 per year for all biological scientists, including gene therapy researchers, in 2016

Number of Jobs
35,110 for all biological scientists in 2016, which includes gene therapy researchers

Future Job Outlook
For biological scientists, which includes gene therapy researchers, predicted to grow 13 percent through 2026

What Does a Gene Therapy Researcher Do?

Genetic diseases are passed on from parents to offspring, and they are caused by genes that have mutated. There are about seven thousand genetic diseases known to science. These include muscular dystrophy, cystic fibrosis, and Parkinson's disease.

A gene therapy researcher (or gene therapist) explores new ways of treating these diseases. Instead of using medications or surgery, he or she deploys the healthy genetic material that is already present in the body's cells. Normal or so-called good genes target those that are not working properly in order to cure the disease or ease its symptoms.

Dr. Jerry Mendell, a researcher working at Nationwide Children's Hospital in Columbus, Ohio, explains the process on the hospital's website: "We take the viral genes out, we put the genes in that we're trying to replace. When we deliver that, it'll go into the target that we want."

The hospital had accepted Tenley Johnson, an infant suffering from a paralyzing, fatal genetic disease, for a clinical trial of a new gene therapy treatment. Dr. Mendell delivered the genes to Tenley with a series of injections. Over time, the treatment proved effective. She began moving her limbs, raising her head, and showing improved muscular strength and agility. She celebrated her second birthday still in the hospital, but alive and improving.

As of early 2018, only three gene therapy procedures had been approved for use in patients. That means gene therapists have a lot of work ahead. They will need to develop new ways of designing and building genes in the lab and introducing them into the body safely. They will have to carry out experiments on ways of editing or building new genes. In designing human clinical trials, they must follow very strict safety standards. The demand for their skills and knowledge will continue to grow.

A gene therapist introduces good genes into the body via a vector, such as a virus, which the therapist uses to infect the patient. But the virus does not cause disease—instead, its purpose is to carry the new gene into the body. Eventually, the body's immune system recognizes the vector as an intruder and destroys it. The new gene survives, however, and spreads as the body's cells reproduce themselves.

One method of putting a mutated gene out of action is called inactivation. The gene therapist introduces a healthy gene that shuts down a mutated gene. This method may work for cancer, a disease in which mutated genes cause damaged cells to replace healthy ones and destroy the function of an organ such as the liver or lungs. New genes that "mark" a cancer cell will trigger the body's own immune system to attack those cells. Marking is a way to get the body's own defenses to work more effectively, and it can spare the patient radiation or chemotherapy treatments that cause nasty side effects such as vomiting, fatigue, and hair loss.

Another, more dangerous strategy is to inject a so-called suicide gene, which produces a toxin that kills the problem cells.

Healthy cells may also be affected, however, causing symptoms that are as bad or worse than those of the original disease.

In augmentation therapy, the gene therapist introduces a new gene that helps a mutated gene to produce an essential protein. In effect, a gene that is not working properly is replaced by a good copy, assisting the body to function normally.

Gene therapy is subject to strict safety guidelines imposed by the US Food and Drug Administration (FDA). Gene therapy researchers must complete long, detailed applications to get any new treatment approved for testing. The agency's guidance document for gene therapy trials comprises twenty-three pages of rules and recommendations.

In their work, gene therapists must carefully balance risks and rewards. If they target the wrong cells, the patient could miss any benefits or contract a new illness. The gene has to be turned on, but this process can be stopped by cells that reject or attack the gene or simply do not react to it. Also, the introduction of new genes can trigger an immune response from the patient that would cause side effects and could be fatal. For that reason, gene therapists must use vectors that do not trigger the immune system.

Some subjects have died while undergoing clinical trials of new gene therapy treatments. Others have come down with leukemia, a dangerous cancer of the body's blood-forming tissues. The field is still controversial among those who oppose any form of manipulation of the human DNA code. Patients in the late stages of a disease who are willing to undergo a new treatment may have their immune systems further compromised, risking new diseases. A new gene that interferes with normal cell division, for example, can trigger cancer. Also, the benefit of any gene therapy treatment may be limited to those in an early stage of the disease.

For all of these methods, gene therapists are studying ways of producing the new genes as efficiently and safely as possible. In so-called ex vivo treatments, cells are removed, exposed to the vector outside the body, allowed to reproduce in the laboratory, and then transplanted back into the body. In vivo treatments, by contrast, treat the cells while they remain in the body—there is no work done on them in the lab.

Gene therapy researchers work at universities or research labs that specialize in this field of medical science. They also work for drug companies that are developing new gene therapy drugs for commercial sale. In August 2017 the FDA approved three gene therapy products—the first to appear on the market. One of these products, Luxturna, treats a form of inherited vision loss caused by a gene mutation. Patients with this disease gradually lose their vision. Luxturna introduces a healthy gene to the cells of the retina, which substantially improves the patient's vision.

Gene therapy researchers are also working on developing treatments for serious diseases such as HIV, cystic fibrosis, hemophilia, Parkinson's disease, and Alzheimer's disease. Although it may not produce a cure, gene therapy may be able to slow or reverse some disease symptoms. Because gene therapy is relatively new, many of these experiments take place on plants and animals. Gene therapists conducting experiments and tests on humans must be medical doctors.

There are challenges with gene therapy products not present in ordinary pharmaceuticals. For example, gene therapists may need to custom-design genes for a patient. Some work with outside labs who create these genes in so-called synthesizers. Although gene synthesis is an extremely expensive and time-consuming process, the technology is becoming less expensive and easier to use. Gene therapists can now edit genes on a laboratory bench, with synthesizers that resemble desktop printers.

How Do You Become a Gene Therapy Researcher?

Education

Whether in the private sector or in education, advanced degrees are essential for any job candidate in this field, and a doctorate is needed for research work. Master's degrees in cellular biology, health sciences, or genetics are relevant, and experience in a scientific or medical laboratory is also key. Many gene therapy researchers also bring a background in molecular biology, cell biology, immunology, biotechnology, or neuroscience.

The field of gene therapy is new and still in an experimental stage. That means the scope and number of job openings is relatively low. Anyone interested in the field can gain experience by winning a fellowship in which the recipient pursues a research project with the support of a university or private institution.

Certification and Licensing

The field of gene therapy has given rise to a debate over restrictions on its use and on experimentation, as well as on licensing of practitioners. As of January 2018, however, no states required licensing specifically for gene therapists. Nor were there any professional certifications available to gene therapists. Anyone administering gene therapy treatments directly to patients, however, must be a licensed doctor.

Internships

Many gene therapy centers offer internships. The Center for Cell and Gene Therapy at Baylor University College of Medicine, for example, stages a summer research internship program that allows students to perform research experiments under the direction of a mentor. Another summer internship in biomedical research is offered at the National Human Genome Research Institute. This program is open to students at all levels, from high school to college. The students benefit from training and mentorship, and they learn about the latest findings of the world's leading genetic researchers. The internship pays a stipend for living expenses.

Skills and Personality

Gene therapy researchers need a strong scientific curiosity and interest in experimental medicine. The field demands researchers who can understand and tolerate the risks involved. Not all gene therapy research has been successful, and at least one clinical trial has resulted in the death of the subject. Patience is also a virtue in the field. Many gene therapy projects fail to produce desired results, and researchers must be prepared to rethink and redo their methods and procedures. Good writing and communication skills are essential for researchers called on to prepare grant applications. This aspect of the job also means drawing up detailed budgets, preparing schedules, and meeting with prospective funders to enlist their support for the research.

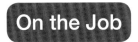

Employers

Gene therapists work for pharmaceutical companies, research institutions, and universities. Some work at hospitals, where they use this new method to treat patients with genetic disorders. Others work independently on research projects funded by government or private-sector grants.

Working Conditions

Gene therapy researchers work mostly in medical laboratories, forming teams dedicated to the development and testing of new drugs and therapies. Because new research is vital to the field, these jobs may demand travel to medical conferences and attendance at lectures or participation in symposia, where other gene therapy specialists describe the details of their work. Gene therapy researchers may also spend their days in testing labs, meeting volunteer subjects, and carefully planning how new drugs and therapies will be administered and how their results will be measured.

Earnings

The field of gene therapy research is so new that the Bureau of Labor Statistics, the federal entity responsible for tracking job statistics, does not break down salary numbers specifically for gene therapy researchers. Among biological scientists, the median annual salary was $74,790 in 2016, with the federal government as the major employer, followed by scientific research groups and colleges and universities.

Opportunities for Advancement

Large companies, universities, and research institutes all offer advancement for gene therapy researchers. With experience, a skilled researcher can move into the job of lab director or head of research. Pharmaceutical firms take a strong interest in new therapies and promote successful researchers to management positions, such as business development director. Advancement would also be open for a gene therapy researcher who specializes in regulatory affairs or the commercial development and marketing of new drugs.

What Is the Future Outlook for Gene Therapy Researchers?

In January 2018, ClinicalTrials.gov listed more than six hundred clinical trials of gene therapies in the United States and abroad. But the risks associated with this new treatment method keep the field limited to experimental research. As of early 2018, the FDA had approved only three drugs for sale. In the future, as the FDA approves new gene therapies, opportunities for researchers will multiply. They will be needed for the design, testing, and improvement of therapies, as well as for designing a safe and reliable manufacturing process for a new generation of medications.

Find Out More

Alliance for Cancer Gene Therapy (ACGT)
96 Cummings Point Rd.
Stamford, CT 06902
http://acgtfoundation.org

This group promotes the use of gene therapy to combat cancer. This application is still in the theoretical stage, so the ACGT is mainly involved with the promotion and funding of lab research and studies. Its website details the work of various clinical researchers across the country.

American Society of Gene and Cell Therapy (ASGCT)
555 E. Wells St., Suite 1100
Milwaukee, WI 53202
www.asgct.org

The ASGCT is the major professional organization for doctors and researchers involved in gene therapy. The organization's website offers news on current research as well as funding opportunities, information on navigating the FDA, a list of gene and cell therapy centers in the United States and abroad, and career-building information for young or new members of the society.

ClinicalTrials.gov
www.clinicaltrials.gov

Part of the US National Library of Medicine, this website lists every medical trial currently ongoing worldwide. Users interested in gene therapy will find a list of gene therapy trials (647 as of January 2018) that include the study title, its status, the conditions treated, the method of intervention, and the location of the trial.

GeneTherapyNet.com
www.genetherapynet.com

An online resource for users seeking professional information on the field of gene therapy. The site provides current news from the field, links to gene therapy societies, and lists of conferences, companies, publications, clinical trials, books, and job openings.

Biostatistician

Biostatistician

Minimum Educational Requirements
Bachelor's degree in math, statistics, public health, or health sciences

Personal Qualities
Skill in handling digital systems and databases; math aptitude; interest in public health issues

Certification and Licensing
Not required

Working Conditions
Indoor at a desk using computer systems and analyzing large sets of numbers, tables, and data

Salary Range
For all mathematicians and statisticians, a median annual salary of $80,500 in 2016

Number of Jobs
40,300 for all statisticians as of 2016

Future Job Outlook
Growth of about 33 percent through 2026

What Does a Biostatistician Do?

Biostatisticians collect and analyze data for use by biologists, agricultural and food scientists, public health agencies, and the medical field. They use the data to study factors impacting the health of people, animals, and plants. Using their knowledge of statistics and computer programs, they design studies to answer pressing questions in the biomedical field.

Biostatisticians work for universities, public health agencies, drug companies, food producers, and federal agencies such as the Centers for Disease Control and Prevention (CDC) and the US Food and Drug Administration (FDA). A group of biostatisticians working together at a university, for example, may seek to understand how well a new medical therapy, such as an experimental surgery, is working. Have patients who underwent the surgery shown side effects? Has their life expectancy improved? How does their lifestyle—their daily routines, what they eat, where they work—affect the results of the procedure? The only way to know is to crunch the numbers and draw conclusions from data collected from the doctors, patients, and hospitals reporting their results.

Drug companies also need biostatisticians. They need to know if new drugs they have developed are effective and safe. This means collecting historical data on the outcome of various therapies and medications already used as well as data on the results of clinical trials. It also may require gathering follow-up data after the drug is placed on the market to understand how it is being used and whether demand is growing from doctors who prescribe the drug.

Regardless of where they are employed, biostatisticians work mostly on computers, employing data-collection-and-analysis software, and often work in teams. They must have a good background in mathematics and statistics. The career demands constant, careful work with large data sets. Biostatisticians have to know how to collect information, analyze it, and explain their findings to other researchers, clients, and the general public.

New medical technologies have raised the demand for biostatisticians. These technologies create data that only advanced computer systems, at the hands of a skilled analyst, can make understandable to doctors, drug manufacturers, and public health officials. A genetic disease, for example, may arise from the mutation of a single gene, but there are more than twenty thousand genes at work in human cells.

A biostatistician assigned to the problem may deal with a mountain of data generated by new gene analyzers in order to track down the hidden source of the disease. The same individual might also access the results of different gene therapies, from thousands of clinical test results, to come up with the most effective treatment.

Biostatisticians are also called on to design research for public health agencies, including the CDC. When a disease outbreak occurs, the CDC works to track down the source. A biostatistician would draw on data from the cities affected by the disease to find correlations. Have there been similar outbreaks in the past? What path is the disease following, and how quickly is it spreading? How are different treatments slowing the disease, if at all?

A biostatistician is responsible for posing and answering these questions.

When a dangerous epidemic occurs, the work of biostatisticians can be a matter of life and death for many people. It can also bring about changes in public policy. During the 1970s, an outbreak of childhood leukemia hit Woburn, Massachusetts. Biostatisticians Marvin Zelen and Stephen Lagakos studied the data, comparing the incidence of disease in Woburn to that in other areas, risk factors such as age and environmental hazards, and the size and location of other recent so-called cancer clusters. Eventually they found a link to the disease in the city's well water, which had long been contaminated with industrial pollutants. This discovery led to the establishment of the Massachusetts Cancer Registry, a database that is now available to researchers studying other outbreaks in other cities.

Biostatistics is also key in plant science, food production, and animal breeding. Seed companies are constantly developing new strains for use by farmers, but they need statisticians to learn how plants respond. That means looking at growth rates, disease rates, and crop yields.

Forestry agencies need studies done on the effects of development, mining, air pollution, and climate change on natural resources. In the outdoors, biostatisticians are also analyzing information on game fish populations, on invasive species such as the zebra mussel, and on the decline in the population of polar bears. They are also studying the population of endangered humpback whales and the effects of an international ban on whale hunting, passed in the early twenty-first century.

How Do You Become a Biostatistician?

Education

To become a biostatistician, students must have at least a bachelor's degree in statistics, biostatistics, or mathematics. Taking part in a statistical research project as an undergraduate is also excellent preparation for a career as a biostatistician. Most jobs in the field of public health will require a master's degree. A master's degree in public health, with a focus on biostatistics, will put graduates on a solid footing in this field.

Many employers look for knowledge of the software and programming languages used by statisticians. This includes SAS, a suite of applications designed to analyze and manipulate data. Electronic data capture is a digital system for capturing data gleaned from clinical trials. Professional biostatisticians have a good knowledge of both tools, and many use them on a daily basis.

Certification and Licensing

There are no licensing requirements for biostatisticians. But those who take part in research involving human subjects may need to be certified as a clinical research professional (CRP). The Association of Clinical Research Professionals and the Society of Clinical Research Associates hold exams required for a CRP certificate.

Internships and Volunteer Work

Many big companies in the health sector, including device makers and pharmaceutical firms, offer summer internships focused on statistical research. Takeda, a pharmaceutical company in Cambridge, Massachusetts, has twelve-week, paid summer internships available for undergraduates, graduate students, and doctoral candidates. Interns work with experienced biostatisticians designing clinical trials and analyzing the results. The Mayo Foundation for Medical Education and Research, Pharmacyclics, Medpace, and Sanford Health all offer biostatistics internships, as do many of the large group health insurers, such as Blue Cross Blue Shield. On its website, the American Statistical Association has a good listing of current internships offered by private companies, as well as public agencies and health departments.

Volunteering in this field will help a jobseeker learn how statistics is applied to real-world issues and problems in the health field. Among the organizations welcoming volunteer biostatisticians are the Peace Corps and Statistics Without Borders (SWB). Founded in 2008, SWB is a group of volunteers who assist clients on a pro bono (free) basis in nonprofit or government agencies focused on health issues.

Skills and Personality

A good head for math and numbers is first among the skills needed by statisticians. Also useful are good problem-solving and critical-thinking skills, the ability to write and speak clearly, and an interest in working on a project team. Biostatisticians must be comfortable with computers and programming and have a strong interest in presenting data sets graphically.

Biostatisticians need to have a geek side; their job means using a lot of different software tools. At one time, workers in this field used Microsoft Excel, a basic spreadsheet program. Now they use more complex and powerful programs, such as DataMelt, Graph-Pad, MedCalc, MaxStat and JMP. Carolyn Ervin, a statistician working for the genomic research company BioRealm, explains on the company's website that "we have many more tools available to us today, not just because new tools have been developed, but even new approaches. We also have so much more computational power and storage available as well. . . . Today we'll often have complex workflows using many different software tools."

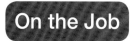

On the Job

Employers

Biostatisticians are needed in public health departments and federal agencies such as the FDA and the CDC. Their skills are in demand in the private sector as well; pharmaceutical and medical equipment manufacturers are constantly surveying the effectiveness of their products. Research institutes, which carry out studies for companies, health systems, and the government, hire statisticians to create these studies and organize the results for their clients. Colleges and universities hire statisticians to teach courses, guide students working on advanced degrees, and develop health surveys. Consulting companies such as Deloitte and Ernst & Young also hire statisticians to provide information and advice to clients in the health care sector.

Working Conditions

Working conditions for biostatisticians are similar to those for other skilled white-collar jobs. Much of their time is spent behind a computer, where they use statistical software to gather and analyze large amounts of raw data. It is common to work in teams under the leadership of a director, who relays project assignments to research associates and assistants. A large project or a pressing deadline may require overtime hours.

Earnings

Median earnings for all mathematicians and statisticians reached $80,500 in 2016. The federal government and professional consulting and research services paid higher wages on average than employers in the education or health care sectors or local government agencies such as county health departments. Holding a master's degree in statistics or public health with a concentration in biostatistics will boost earning power.

Opportunities for Advancement

Statistics has applications across the entire spectrum of the health care field. With experience, a biostatistician can be promoted to head of a data analytics department or move into the ranks of management at hospitals, pharmaceutical companies, or medical device makers, all of whom depend on a good understanding of their data to provide products and services. Statistics is advancing to a key academic study as well, and biostatisticians have opportunities to hold professorships and fellowships, or pursue research projects, at colleges and universities.

What Is the Future Outlook for Biostatisticians?

The biostatistician career holds a promising future. Sources of statistical data—on health, medicines, and related areas—are expanding quickly. As more and more data becomes available, the demand for the people with the talent to analyze it and make it understandable, will rise. "I've been telling people that the really sexy job . . . is to be a statistician," declares Hal Varian, Google's chief economist. "They're the people that can make the data tell its story, and everybody has data." Google has hundreds of statisticians, Varian adds in a YouTube interview, but that is still not enough to deal with all the data this single company generates. For all mathematicians and statisticians, the Bureau of Labor Statistics predicts a job growth rate of 33 percent through 2026 — faster by a long way than growth for most other careers.

Find Out More

American Statistical Association (ASA)
732 N. Washington St.
Alexandria, VA 22314
www.amstat.org

In the careers section of its website, the ASA provides useful information for anyone interested in a future as a statistician. There are lists of fellowships and grants, ethical guidelines, salary information, and a JobWeb listing current openings. Under the education tab, there are links to competitions, courses, internships, and community programs.

International Society for Clinical Biostatistics
Bregnerodvej 132
DK-3460 Birkerod
Denmark
www.iscb.info

Based in Denmark, this society welcomes members from many different fields, including pharmacologists, chemists, statisticians, and clinicians. As an international group, it holds conferences and workshops all over the world to exchange ideas and instruct biostatisticians in the latest methods and theories in the field.

National Center for Health Statistics
1600 Clifton Rd.
Atlanta, GA 30329
www.cdc.gov/nchs

Maintained by the CDC, the center maintains the federal government's massive database of health statistics. Its website describes how biostatisticians collect, analyze, and write about their numbers. It also highlights stats on current issues, such as prescription opioid abuse, and features the Data Visualization Gallery, where data is rendered in a variety of graphs, charts, heat maps, and tables.

University of California, Los Angeles (UCLA)
Department of Biostatistics
650 Charles E. Young Dr. South
51-254 CHS
Los Angeles, CA 90095
www.biostat.ucla.edu

This website introduces the graduate biostatistics department at UCLA, with useful descriptions of the degree programs and courses, prospective careers, and current job opportunities at the school. Studying this page will give anyone interested in postgraduate work in biostatistics an idea of what these programs offer, both in education and in career guidance.

Pharmaceutical Engineer

At a Glance

Pharmaceutical Engineer

Minimum Educational Requirements
Bachelor's degree in a science-related field, including health sciences, biology, chemistry, or engineering

Personal Qualities
Skill in handling chemical formulas and analysis; interest in process engineering; interest in health care

Certification and Licensing
Certification as an engineer specializing in pharmaceuticals may be required by some employers

Working Conditions
Indoors, working in pharmaceutical labs, manufacturing complexes, and/or testing facilities

Salary Range
Chemical engineers, including pharmaceutical engineers, earned a median annual salary of $98,340 in 2016

Number of Jobs
32,700 for all chemical engineers, which includes pharmaceutical engineers

Future Job Outlook
About 8 percent growth through 2026 for all chemical engineers, including pharmaceutical engineers

What Does a Pharmaceutical Engineer Do?

A pharmaceutical engineer is in the business of making medicines. There are many steps along the road to bringing a new drug to market, and drug companies need skilled engineers with a deep knowledge of the drug manufacturing process to navigate that journey.

Some pharmaceutical engineers design drugs. They develop the chemical formulas and the recipes for adding, mixing, and finally assembling medications into their final form. Others specialize in the clinical trials that will allow a new drug to pass the requirements of the US Food and Drug Administration (FDA). They observe the effects that different forms and doses of a new drug have on test subjects and write up reports explaining their findings. These reports are submitted to sponsoring companies and to the FDA, which must give permission for the sale of both prescription and over-the-counter medications.

The work of pharmaceutical engineers is key during the earliest phase of new drug production. To work effectively, they must have a deep knowledge of biology and chemistry. They rely on research and data on the effectiveness of chemicals to treat certain diseases.

The process begins when pharmaceutical engineers identify molecules that are causing disease. In many cases the suspect is a protein present in the blood or other tissues. The disease-causing agent is put through a screening process in which engineers apply different chemical compounds that might be effective in blocking its action. Each drug company has a big library of these compounds held in storage, either physically in a lab or in the form of designs kept in a computerized database. Compounds found to be effective against the targeted disease—known as hits—are then further tested to ensure they work consistently against the disease in a laboratory. The process continues with animal testing. The research then continues to clinical trials on human beings.

The discovery process can take years and requires a huge financial investment by the company. To do their job effectively, pharmaceutical engineers need an expert knowledge in how specific diseases develop. They must know whether a disease is caused by a virus or a bacterium, whether it is contagious, and whether it is a genetic illness passed down from parents to offspring. They need to know how certain chemicals slow down the disease or help the body eliminate it. They also must be aware of possible side effects and whether a certain chemical formula might be dangerously toxic.

At the pharmaceutical company Roche, engineer Mary Mallaney works in the purification development department. In an interview Roche posted on YouTube, Mallaney describes her role at the company:

> Each new molecule that they want to put into clinical trials, they give it to us, so the things I do day to day support the development of those materials and support delivering into the pipeline to the patient. I'm responsible for different

experiments to figure out how to make this step work the best it can, figure out how to remove the impurities. . . . I need to be rushing around and doing as many of these experiments as I can so we can produce the material as quickly as we can.

Pharmaceutical engineers can also draw on discoveries from the natural world. Many plants produce chemical compounds that can be used to treat human ailments and disease. Kersch Naidoo, an engineer working at South Africa's Council for Scientific and Industrial Research (CSIR), is studying a native plant for its effects on health. In an interview with CSIR New Media posted on YouTube, he describes a current project: "One of the products I'm involved in is optimizing the extraction of the active ingredient in African ginger. We are currently working on cough syrup as well as a cream and a lotion that uses the extract."

Before it was brought into the lab, African ginger was an important herbal medicine among the Zulu people of South Africa, used for everything from nausea to poor digestion to bad breath. Many pharmaceutical engineers specialize in the development of commercial remedies from plants, a process that has contributed many drugs, including aspirin, to modern medicine.

A pharmaceutical engineer may also be responsible for the drug manufacturing process. After small batches of a drug are used for clinical trials and the drug is approved for sale, the company needs to scale up production to supply the expected market. A pharmaceutical engineer designs and oversees this work. He or she may also be involved in the design and packaging of the drug.

If production moves to new factories, which may be overseas, pharmaceutical engineers are responsible for ensuring the consistency, safety, and quality of the product. If demand for the product decreases, they are also responsible for a scale-down process.

In some cases, they need to figure out how to safely use toxic chemical or biological compounds. The cosmetological drug Botox, for example, is made from tiny amounts of botulinum—a dangerous biological agent that causes deadly food poisoning. Pharmaceutical engineers figured out how to derive Botox from this agent, how to handle it safely in the manufacturing process, and how to package and transport it securely and in the correct doses.

Pharmaceutical engineers have many different job titles. Those working to develop new drugs are often known as research and development specialists or managers. Others are quality assurance managers, who make sure that drug development and manufacturing meet federal safety guidelines. A quality assurance manager's duties include inspecting factories, research labs, and testing sites. Process engineers direct the work of technicians and equipment in a factory. Quality control analysts are responsible for making sure drugs are made consistently and according to formula. They create standard operating procedures for the manufacturing process. They also carry out tests to make sure the drugs are meeting quality standards.

How Do You Become a Pharmaceutical Engineer?

Education

To enter the field of pharmaceutical engineering, applicants need at least a bachelor of science degree with a major in a subject relevant to the field, such as biology or chemistry. Employers seeking research and development engineers may require advanced degrees in pharmaceutical science or chemical engineering.

Many universities offer degree programs in pharmaceutical engineering. Some of these programs serve as pipelines to private companies and public agencies seeking new and experienced talent in the field. Rutgers University, for example, has close ties to New Jersey's large pharmaceutical industry, and it allows higher-level undergraduates to attend graduate-level courses in its pharmaceutical engineering program.

Certification and Licensing

There are no licensing requirements by the states or the federal government specifically for pharmaceutical engineers. But certification as a professional engineer is available through two

Pharmaceutical engineers play an important role in developing and evaluating new medicines. Some specialize in developing new formulas for medications while others monitor how well the new drugs work in clinical trials.

examinations, the second of which covers an emphasis such as chemical or biomedical engineering. An employer may require professional engineer licensure for its pharmaceutical engineering applicants.

The International Society for Pharmaceutical Engineering certifies candidates for the title of pharmaceutical industry professional. Applicants may be anyone working in the industry, and the credential must be renewed every three years.

Internships and Volunteer Work

Many companies offer paid or unpaid internships to students interested in a future career in pharmaceutical engineering. The California company Pharmacyclics, for example, hires science majors to assist in its development of new cancer drugs. The interns learn to operate lab equipment, prepare tissue samples, handle computer software and medical data, and assist in the development of new lab procedures. This kind of an internship offers valuable hands-on experience in a commercial pharmaceutical lab.

Volunteer opportunities are common at hospitals, clinics, and public health departments. A volunteer may help patients with paperwork or nurses with testing procedures. He or she may become familiar with how drugs are administered or how a clinic handles them while also learning the ins and outs of patient assistance programs that help with the price of medications. A volunteer in such a setting will come away with direct contact with patients and professional staff and a deeper understanding of how the pharmaceutical industry interacts with physicians and facilities that represent the marketplace for pharmaceutical products.

Skills and Personality

Pharmaceutical engineers need a good understanding of mathematics and scientific logic, as well as excellent problem-solving skills. They should be active learners who can digest new information and understand new problems and breakthroughs in their field. They also must have good written and spoken communication skills, including the ability to work with others to solve complex problems in drug research, manufacturing, and safety. A sense of scientific curiosity also helps, as pharmaceutical companies are constantly on the hunt for new medications, new methods of manufacturing their products, and creative ways of delivering them to the market.

Employers

Pharmaceutical engineers are in demand at pharmaceutical companies as well as research labs and universities that carry out the work of creating new drug therapies. Federal agencies such as the National Institutes of Health and the FDA also hire these specialists. Many pharmaceutical engineers find employment with nonprofit companies, which supply medications to poor and developing countries where big pharmaceutical companies choose not to market their products.

Working Conditions

A common job setting for a pharmaceutical engineer is a science lab. In the lab, they use computers and measuring and mixing equipment to develop new drug formulas and manufacturing processes. They may spend time in so-called clean labs, where filters and air pumps eliminate dust, chemical vapors, and airborne microbes. In these sterile environments they carry out research and clinical tests. Or they may work on a factory floor supervising production workers and machinery.

Earnings

The salary for pharmaceutical engineers varies by company and by job description. A survey published online by the job-search site Glassdoor, for example, found an annual salary of $119,792 for a pharmaceutical engineer at one company in Parsippany, New Jersey, and $39 per hour for the same job at another company in Lancaster, Pennsylvania. The Bureau of Labor Statistics (BLS) does not identify pharmaceutical engineer as an occupation separate from chemical engineer. The BLS found a median annual salary of $97,940 for chemical engineers working in pharmaceutical manufacturing.

Opportunities for Advancement

With experience, a pharmaceutical engineer can move into the management ranks of a pharmaceutical company, where knowledge of the drug development and manufacturing process is essential. Experienced pharmaceutical engineers can also move into university-level teaching positions in the subjects of chemistry, biology, or medicine, and research institutes will hire experienced pharmaceutical engineers to develop studies on new therapies that could potentially have commercial applications.

What Is the Future Outlook for Pharmaceutical Engineers?

The pharmaceutical industry continues to grow. According to one survey, it is projected to reach $1 trillion in global sales by 2020. That means commercial research and development departments will see increased funding and will have an increased need for capable engineers. In addition, the industry is branching into several new methods of drug delivery, including biologic drugs and gene therapies. These advances will increase the demand for pharmaceutical engineers with relevant experience in these specialized areas.

New and start-up pharmaceutical companies have become major businesses in developing countries, particularly in India and other parts of Asia. The aging of populations in the United States, Europe, and East Asia means pharmaceutical companies will be catering to a larger market. The occurrence of global disease outbreaks, such as the bird flu, also stimulates public demand for new pharmaceutical products. The ability to scale up and manage drug manufacturing will be an in-demand skill around the world.

Find Out More

International Society for Pharmaceutical Engineering
7200 Wisconsin Ave., Suite 305
Bethesda, MD 20814
www.ispe.org

This nonprofit group offers education, training, conferences, and journals, all in support of the pharmaceutical engineering and manufacturing field. The society's website provides news on the trending issues in the industry, including data integrity, drug toxicity, safe manufacturing guidelines, and gene therapies.

Pharmaceutical Manufacturing
www.pharmamanufacturing.com

With a wealth of information, this website keeps visitors up-to-date on topics important to pharmaceutical engineers: new products and processes, information technology, quality assurance, and compliance with the government's many rules and regulations. There is also a resource directory, a section for webinars, and a career center.

ProClinical Life Sciences Recruitment Blog
https://blog.proclinical.com

Produced by a company that recruits new employees in the life sciences, this blog features various articles for hopeful applicants, including "How to Get a Job as a Chemical Engineer in the Pharmaceutical Industry." The post gives a concise explanation of how to prepare for a career as a pharmaceutical engineer.

US Food and Drug Administration (FDA)
10903 New Hampshire Ave.
Silver Spring, MD 20993
https://www.fda.gov

This federal agency regulates drug manufacturing and sales, and provides guidance for all pharmaceutical research in the United States. The website has information on current FDA activities in the regulation of drugs, vaccines, cosmetics, tobacco, and many other products.

Interview with a Genetic Counselor

Heather Zierhut is a genetic counselor with eight years of experience working with children with rare genetic diseases and currently is the associate director of a master of genetic counseling graduate program at the University of Minnesota, Twin Cities. In an e-mail interview with the author, she discussed her experiences in the field.

Q: Why did you become a genetic counselor?

A: I had investigated a lot of professions, including medicine, basic science research, veterinary medicine, and nothing seemed to fit until I heard about genetic counseling. As a genetic counselor, I could investigate the genetic causes of disease (research), teach people about their conditions (education), and help them make decisions or adapt to their circumstances (counsel). The combination of all of these things and being able to directly work with patients was what drew me to the profession.

Q: Can you describe your typical workday?

A: One of the best things about being a genetic counselor is that my day is never typical. In general, no two days are ever the same. In general, genetic counselors use their unique skills to effectively communicate complicated genetic information in an understandable and [empathetic] manner. Whether working in a clinic answering difficult patient questions or in a laboratory writing genetic testing reports, many of the skills are the same.

Q: What do you like most about your job?

A: One of my favorite parts of my job is when a patient has an "aha" moment. This moment could be when they learn something that is important to them or their family, when they are able [to] access resources to help them make a decision, or when they can better manage their condition. In some cases, a patient may simply have an answer to a question [for which] they never knew the answer. In clinic, I had the opportunity to see some patients for years. And in these cases, I was a part of their journey. I saw them during some of their toughest times. This part of my job, although at times challenging and hard, was ultimately the most rewarding part of being a genetic counselor.

Q: What do you like least about your job?
A: Paperwork, paperwork, paperwork.

Q: What personal qualities do you find most valuable for this type of work?
A: Because there are always new discoveries being made in genetics, the job never stays the same. Someone thinking about being a genetic counselor should have a natural curiosity for science and be a lifelong learner. Being a genetic counselor also requires flexibility. Each patient is different, and circumstances change. Genetic counselors have to be centered on the patient and their needs, which requires them to be able to listen to their patients' needs.

Q: What is the best way to prepare for this type of job?
A: If you can shadow a genetic counselor or watch a video of a genetic counseling session, it will show you what really happens in a session. This demystifies the process and also shows the challenging nature of some of the topics that genetic counselors [face], such as a diagnosis of cancer, a baby with a congenital anomaly, or a child with a rare genetic condition. Second, get experience in advocacy. Try volunteering for a crisis counseling line, working at a hospital, or tutoring children with learning difficulties.

Q: What other advice do you have for students who might be interested in this career?
A: There are lots of different types of jobs that genetic counselors can do in clinical (cancer, prenatal, cardiology, neurology), industry (laboratory, marketing, sales), public health (newborn screening, telegenetics), and other settings (nonprofits). The degree gives you a world of options. Once you have a genetic counseling degree, you can choose what is best for you.

Other Jobs in Biotechnology

Biochemist
Biophysicist
Bioproduction operator
Cell biologist
Clinical research associate
Contract and grant analyst
Entomologist
Environmental safety consultant
Epidemiologist
Forensic DNA analyst
Greenhouse technician
Health and safety engineer
Immunologist
Laboratory animal technician
Laboratory director

Laboratory geneticist
Medical device engineer
Medical scientist
Packaging specialist
Parasitologist
Pharmaceutical sales
    representative
Process materials handler
Product testing engineer
Public health specialist
Quality assurance engineer
Regulatory affairs specialist
Research animal caretaker
Validation specialist
Zoologist

Editor's note: The US Department of Labor's Bureau of Labor Statistics provides information about hundreds of occupations. The agency's *Occupational Outlook Handbook* describes what these jobs entail, the work environment, education and skill requirements, pay, future outlook, and more. The *Occupational Outlook Handbook* may be accessed online at www.bls.gov/ooh.

Index